Men's Guide to High-Conflict Divorce

- a guide from –

T Fitz

Dedication

This book is dedicated to all the good dads out there who have been steamrolled by conflict seeking women and the family court system. Also, to my dad, Donny, who lost the war to cancer in 2012. And most importantly, to my son, Zeke, without whom I would have no reason to breathe.

ACKNOWLEDGMENT

Thanks to my second wife, the mother of my son. Without her blatant lies and particular brand of crazy, I wouldn't have the experience to write this guide. C'est la vie!

CONTENTS

Introduction

For all my brothers from other mothers out there who are considering marriage, for the ones trapped in one, and for the ones already aware their marriage is over; I present you with this guide. High-conflict divorce is no joke and not to be taken lightly. For you, I will lay out the process and some guidance to help you traverse what will be a long and rough road.

It is said that all marriages end: half in divorce and half in death, but all marriages end. I believe the 50% divorce rate to be a lowball estimate, but we'll go with it. No divorces are easy, although some are non-contested. For those, you are still left with heartache, but should you be in that situation, count your lucky stars, as a contested divorce is a battle. It is an open declaration of war and should be taken as such. I believe approximately 70% of divorces are initiated by the wife. This was true for my first marriage, which was ended by my first wife in 2010. That divorce was a cakewalk compared to the next.

I ended my second marriage, the inspiration for this guide, and can now count myself in the 30% of men that divorce their wives. It was highly contested, and our newborn son was involved. To this day, the dust has not settled. I'll do my best to guide you through the process, but first let me tell you how it began; the abbreviated version.

I was a beta simpanzee. I took in a woman who was trying to kick the needle. A woman who had years before promised me she wanted to be barefoot in the kitchen but changed her mind to get back to her drug of choice, Opana, generically known as Oxymorphone, one of the strongest opiates you will find. She had been calling me for years, using me as an emotional tampon, telling me of the abuse she was suffering. Once, she had just left the latest "abuser" when another ex of hers was stabbed. Some drug deal had gone wrong, and she ran to his rescue where they enjoyed vein popping methamphetamines. As the story goes, he kicked her in the head, neighbors heard the commotion and contacted law enforcement. The man was arrested and ended up with a battery charge.

That's when I allowed her to come stay at my residence, another horrible mistake in a long list that started when I fell for the barefoot in the kitchen line and allowed myself to be her emotional tampon for years. I can't tell you the number of mistakes I've made at this point; that count has been lost along the way. I will tell you the red flags were obviously there, and I should have used that information in my personal decision-making process. Regardless, I didn't, and she was now my visitor.

At this time she was at, or near, rock bottom. It was late December and I vowed she could stay for two weeks and then must depart. I allowed her to stay longer; another mistake. She gave me the story of being barefoot in the kitchen again and how she wanted to start a family, and I took the bait. I did end up with a beautiful baby boy, whom I love dearly, but I also got a lot more than I initially bargained for. I am barely able to see my son and have been turned into nothing more than a wallet, but hindsight is 20/20.

It's been a hard and arduous process, but I'll guide you through it and at least let you know what to expect. I'll also give you all the early warning signs of high-conflict and touch on emotional abuse, as well as some of the best advice the first attorney I contacted imparted upon me. Then with the power of hindsight, I'll tell you what I would have done if I had everything to do over again. Too bad that's not the way this life works. In life, you get one shot. Make sure to aim well!

Personality disorders

Only a licensed professional can diagnose a personality disorder, and I am no licensed professional, but I would say most, if not all high-conflict divorces can be tied to some disorder of personality. There are 10 formally recognized ones, but there are two in particular the reader may want to become familiar with. Borderline Personality Disorder (BPD) and Narcissistic Personality Disorder (NPD).

We'll start with BPD, which impacts the way one thinks and feels about themselves and others causing problems functioning in everyday life. It includes self-image issues, along with difficulty managing emotion and behavior. These traits then lead the sufferer into a pattern of unstable relationships. If you notice this red flag, take heed. This person may have an intense fear of abandonment or instability, along with difficulty tolerating being by themselves. Those with BPD will also often possess low emotional intelligence. Many think those with BPD lack empathy, however this is not true. They can empathize, but the intensity of their own emotions tends to render them oblivious to the emotions of those around them. They're like a drowning person who grabs a would-be rescuer and pulls them both down.

Those with BPD will often show impulsive aggression when they become overwhelmed and, although they may seem as mature as any other adult in certain situations, when it comes to coping with strong emotions, they are often stuck at a child's developmental level.

There are five areas of contention that will arise in almost any relationship with a person afflicted with BPD.

There will be the "it's your fault" fight, when they won't be able to take any responsibility for their current situation. If they were able to see fault in themselves, they would no longer be perfect, and therefore defective.

Then you have the "heads I win, tails you lose" fight. This is when they place you in a no win scenario. One of those that, no matter what you say or what logic you bring up, you still lose.

Then there is the "projection" fight. This is when they project their own feelings or insecurities onto you. For instance, your spouse may be having an affair or even just lustful thoughts and will then project that onto you through accusations of you doing the same. I never once cheated on my wife, but I always had a gut feeling she may have been screwing around. Almost every Friday like clockwork, I would be accused of infidelity when I got home from playing golf, while she had been running around town. I still wonder about that. Then again, you just gotta learn to let go to move on.

The "I hate you, don't leave me" fight occurs when they distance themselves to avoid feeling controlled, but then feel neglected, so they try to get closer again. Rinse and repeat.

And finally, the "testing" fight, when they will throw all sorts of shit tests your way in an attempt to gauge how you really feel about them. Whole books are written on the subject. If you are interested in learning more, you will find a plethora of resources online.

Along with BPD, you will also want to familiarize yourself with NPD. There are all sorts of NPD, from covert to overt and more, but they all have some of the same underlying issues and patterns, including lack of empathy and a sense of entitlement. Relationships with persons conflicted with NPD can be broken down into phases. The first phase is referred to as *Love Bombing*. This is the time during which they cause you to fall madly in love by making themselves into what they believe you see as the perfect mate. Who wouldn't want to be with a person they perceived as perfect? They're going to figure you out and become that person. You must stay on your toes and pay attention should this materialize.

The *Love Bombing* phase is followed by *Devalue and Discard*. After they've hooked you and reeled you in, they are going to start changing it up and become manipulative. They will gaslight you making you begin to question your own sense of reality. Watch out for the gaslighting! I was put through so much of it; I knew something was wrong; I knew this person was playing me through manipulative lies and I saw straight through it, yet I did nothing. Don't let that be you.

They will start to isolate you from your support network of friends and family, then blame you, shame you, threaten you, guilt-trip you, and withhold things from you such as money, sex, or their time while making demands of you. They may become sarcastic about you in front of others to put you "in your place," lowering your self-esteem while they themselves sit smugly with an appearance of superiority.

During this phase you will find yourself making excuses for their behavior. Partially because you have become so enamored during the love bombing phase, but also because they will keep throwing a little love bombing into the mix, keeping you on your toes, making you think that perfect companion is still somewhere in there. You may start feeling like you live in a fog of confusion and are forever walking on eggshells trying to appease the person who once made you feel incredibly special.

The narcissist is quite selfish; always looking at what's in it for them. At the beginning it may have been the prestige of dating you, money or even just the chase. This is where they gain the narcissistic supply they need to fuel their ego, but once they have sucked you dry, and you no longer give them this supply, you will enter the next phase of the relationship: *Discard*.

They will discard you like an old pair of holey socks and replace you with an upgraded model they can use as a new source of narcissistic supply.

At this point, one of two things will happen. If you are lucky, they will leave you alone. This will only happen if they feel they've caused you enough emotional pain to validate themselves. Sick right? I know. If they don't leave you alone, they will try to start reeling you back in. This is called *Hoovering*. Yeah, like the vacuum. If you fall into this trap, the narcissistic relationship cycle continues. You got it, back to stage one; prepare yourself for some *Love Bombing*, leading right back to *Devalue*, then *Discard*, on to *Hoovering*. This cycle will continue to repeat, most likely in shorter intervals, until the narcissist has completely destroyed you or you have somehow removed them from your life.

If you find yourself in a relationship with this type of person, it's important that you find a way out. The bad news is that it won't be easy. I can nonetheless attest that no matter how hard it may be getting yourself out of the relationship, your life will end up much worse should you stay.

If you can see any of these characteristics in your high-conflict ex-partner, you are not alone. There are many resources online as well as communities that can help provide the support you need to get your life back on track. Maybe search YouTube. There are plenty of channels related to the topic. Here are some that helped me get perspective: *Surviving Narcissism*, *DSD* and *Rebecca Zung*. It is sad, but there are many out there, just like you, who found themselves in a trap laid by someone with one of these personality disorders. I urge you to find the help you need.

Emotional Abuse

Something that will undoubtedly have happened during your marriage to a high-conflict person, whether that person has an actual disorder of personality or not, is emotional abuse. Physical abuse, that may have also occurred, leaves signs on the outside for others to see, but the scars from emotional abuse reside inside us. It may take a very long time, therapy, and a good support group to overcome the effects of prolonged emotional abuse, but you have to do what it takes for yourself and those you love. You can do it! We'll go over some of the signs and hopefully offer some insight into the steps you can take to recovery.

Emotional abuse is a way for another person to control you. A lot of this comes down to control. They accomplish this using emotions to criticize, embarrass, shame, blame or otherwise manipulate you. This could happen from time to time in any relationship, but it becomes abuse when a consistent pattern of this behavior emerges. Emotional abuse is not only relegated to romantic relationships, but can occur in any relationship, even those among friends, family members and co-workers. In hindsight, I was emotionally abusive towards my first wife without even knowing it. I will say however, that the emotional abuse I put my first wife through was not nearly as bad as it can get in other relationships. It came from how I was raised, which I must say, in no way justifies any sort of abuse. Luckily, through much self reflection I saw my actions as wrong and corrected them over time. This, however disdainful, did help me come to know the hallmarks of these patterns and to understand when abusive behavior was being levied towards myself.

After enough of this abuse, you may start to feel trapped; often too wounded to endure the relationship any longer, but also afraid to leave. Unfortunately, the cycle will repeat itself until something is done. Let's discuss this a little further so I can give you some idea of what you can do to safely get yourself out of an abusive relationship.

To determine if you are in an abusive relationship, you must take time to examine it. Emotional abuse can be difficult to detect. If you are having trouble making a determination, stop and think about how interactions with this person make you feel. Yep, we have to dig into those feelings. It can be difficult for many men, as we often want to suppress our feelings, but trust me, you must. Dive into those emotions. See what's there. You'll be a stronger individual for it. Self-knowledge is paramount to living your best life.

Emotionally abusive people will display unrealistic expectations. These can come in the form of unreasonable demands, expecting you to put their needs first, being dissatisfied no matter how hard you try or how much you give, criticizing the way you accomplish normal tasks, not allowing you to have your own opinions, and demanding you name exact dates and times when discussing things that upset you.

They will invalidate you. This can be through undermining, dismissing, or distorting your perceptions of reality, refusing to accept your feelings, requiring you to explain how you feel over and over, accusing you of being too sensitive, emotional, or crazy. They may dismiss your requests, wants, and needs as ridiculous, suggest your perceptions are wrong or that you cannot be trusted, stating that you blow things out of proportion. They accuse you of being selfish, needy, or materialistic if you express your wants or needs and will have the expectation that you should not have these wants or needs.

The emotional abuser will create chaos in your life. They accomplish this by starting arguments just for the sake of arguing, making confusing and contradictory statements, having drastic mood changes or sudden emotional outbursts. They may nitpick your clothing, hair, work, or basically anything about you. They can behave so erratically and unpredictably that you feel like you constantly have to be very careful not to set them off. Yep, those old eggshells again.

They will use emotional blackmail. This comes in the form of manipulating and controlling you, making you feel guilty, humiliating you in public, as well as in private. They will use your fears, values, compassions, or other hot buttons to control you or the situation. They may exaggerate your flaws, which we all have, or just point them out in order to deflect attention to avoid taking responsibility for their poor decisions or mistakes. They will often gaslight you, denying that an event took place or just lying about it. They will also punish you by withholding affection or something else you may value, very much like you see in the personality disorders we previously discussed.

They may control you through isolation. Getting you away from your friends, family and your support network makes the job of controlling you much easier. They may go through your phone on a regular basis. I know my last wife did this, and although there was nothing there to be mad about, I hated it because each time it would lead to a fight. Yep, an argument just for the sake of arguing.

When emotional abuse is severe and ongoing, it comes with dire consequences for the victim. They may lose their sense of self and start to become critical of themselves believing they are not worth the air they breathe. Over time, the accusations, name-calling, criticisms, and gaslighting erode the victim's sense of self so much that they can no longer see themselves realistically. They may even begin to agree with the abuser. Once this happens, most victims become trapped in the abusive relationship believing they will never be good enough for anyone else.

Sustained emotional abuse can even lead to disorders of body and mind. It can cause depression and anxiety, stomach ulcers, heart palpitations, eating disorders, and insomnia. This is why it is so critical that you find a way out of the abusive relationship.

I am unable to offer you legal advice, I'm not a lawyer, but I can tell you that emotional abuse is illegal and there is someone in your area that is there to help you. For me, it was a women's advocate. I know that seems counterintuitive, but she wasn't there just for women. She was there to help anyone suffering through an abusive relationship. I only wish I had met her sooner, before what we will discuss in the next section occurred. Your advocate will be able to assist you in getting a temporary order of protection where the abuser will have to leave the residence and cease contact with you, normally for a minimum of three months. Should they contact you, all it will take is one report to get them arrested. This will give you time and a paper trail to start putting your life back together. Your advocate will also be able to guide you in seeking the therapy that you may very well need, in order to get your mental state back in order. Don't believe going to therapy makes you weak; it takes a strong person to go to therapy.

If you are in this situation, or have a loved one who is, I hope this has helped give some insight to the situation and some guidance on how to find a remedy.

False Allegations and Orders of Protection

It's a sad reality and unfortunately one our court system doesn't have the tools and understanding at this point to properly deal with, but if you're wrapped up in a high-conflict divorce or custody case, you need to be prepared for false allegations. The chances are very high that the other side will lie to paint you as some sort of heinous villain. Unfounded allegations of domestic violence, substance abuse, sexual abuse and child molestation are quite common. It has been shown that at least 70, and up to 90 percent of the time when children are involved, false allegations will be levied against the other party. Talk to any attorney who has represented people in high-conflict divorce and custody cases; they'll attest that false allegations are prevalent.

Women have a huge advantage in today's family court system and allegations of this nature are known among attorneys as the nuclear weapon of divorce. You may think your ex would never do this sort of thing to you, and hopefully you are right, however you'd be surprised at the lengths a high-conflict person will go to metaphorically bury you. If you'd like to read some of these stories, get yourself a copy of *Destructive Lies* by Melissa McFadden. There you can read "True Stories of Them Too", about people and those who love them whose lives were absolutely ruined by false allegations.

Check out DadsDivorce.com and their founder Joseph Cordell. He writes about the abuse of a system designed to protect against abuse in a Huffington Post article, *"Order of Protection: And Justice for All?"*. Cordell states that "Time and time again, I have seen orders of protection treat the man like a criminal when there is no basis for the endangerment claims. These men are law-abiding citizens and great fathers who see their rights challenged or completely vanish in court."

Psychology Today notes that one of the trends they are seeing in the era of #MeToo is false allegations of abuse or assault made by an angry, irrational and spiteful spouse. They admit, as do I, that many allegations made are true and proven and those should be taken seriously, but there are also false allegations that are made in spite to "win" a legal battle or custody of the children, or worse, to get "even" by completely destroying the other spouse. They further state that certain people are more at risk of making these types of allegations and then give an explanation of BPD. That's one reason I thought it prudent to bring up personality disorders in an earlier section.

These reasons highlight the importance of learning about emotional abuse and speaking with an advocate if you believe you could ever find yourself in this situation. You will need that order of protection to help you in the war of high-conflict divorce. I'm definitely not suggesting you apply for protection if it is not warranted, but if it is, I would recommend applying. Orders of protection are granted *ex-parte*, meaning the person granting it doesn't even speak with the other party. For women, these orders are quite easy to obtain. All they have to do is say they feel threatened and whammo, order granted. The system has a long way to go before it can be considered a process that dispenses actual justice.

The sad part is that those who manufacture false allegations are devaluing the claims from the people who have actually been victims of domestic violence and/or sexual assault. Absolutely heartbreaking.

Legal Counsel: You're Life-Jacket

If you find yourself in the throes of a high-conflict divorce, you're going to need an attorney. A good attorney. Acquiring the right attorney is key and a quite difficult task. The bad news is that a good attorney is going to cost you a lot of money. Many of us may not have that kind of cash. If that is you, I would first do everything I could to find financing somehow, but if you just can't you will have to proceed pro se (meaning you are your own attorney).

For the pro se route, you will have a lot of learning to do. This will fill all of your free time. You will have to learn about the law, motions and how to properly draft them. You will have to learn how to file them and who to file them with. Timeframes will also be very important. It still floors me at how much information a person must digest to be able to properly represent themselves in our family court system.

Whether you decide to take the pro se route or not, there are a few things you need to know. The legal system says there is no discrimination against men, but let me tell you the courts' actions don't back up their claim. You are going to need to start reading the family code of your state, as well as some of the federal laws and statutes. Watch YouTube videos of others who have gone through these same ordeals and shared their stories. Find a community to bounce ideas off and offer you support through this tough time. You will find this information and support to be invaluable. It's going to take up a lot of your evenings, but if you love your kids, you need to put in the effort for them. High-conflict women don't make good mothers, so your kids are going to need you to fight, and you need to know how.

If you decide to hire an attorney, make sure to interview at least three of them. You are going to need to ask about expectations regarding results in the particular court in which you will be appearing. If an attorney is honest, they will tell you about the ugly side of the situation you face. Other than expectations you will need to ask about billing.

Many attorneys will quote you a flat rate, only for you to later find out that the flat rate was just a retainer that they expect to run out so they can begin charging you $200-$500 per hour. You need to know how those hours are billed. For instance, do they charge 0.25 hours per email or 0.50 hours per email? Emailing your attorney can get expensive, and often they don't actually read the words you have placed in front of them, trust me on this.

Let's talk about a better approach to the chain of emails. In preparation for your hearings, make sure to schedule weekly or bi-weekly, 30 minute meetings with your attorney via Zoom, or in person. This will help keep you on the same page, and you'll end up spending less than if you had sent them everything you will discuss in your meeting via email. Also record these meetings so you will have a record. You can't predict the future but documentation of the past is your friend.

Make sure your attorney keeps you abreast of expectations. Many just want to ride out the billable hours and not do any real preparation, just to wing it in court. You can't let this happen. Get your witnesses in line and have them meet with your attorney. You need to know your attorney's strategy throughout the process. Stay informed, it is a must.

You must be diligent about gathering any evidence you have that may help you. You may even find your attorney tells you the judge won't care about some of the evidence you believe would result in a slam dunk. This is a rough area, but you can nevertheless insist it be submitted into evidence. If not submitted, it is useless during the appeals process.

Learn about appeals. There are certain things that must happen in court to be able to make it to the appellate court. For instance, if the other side submits evidence, you must object on a certain ground or you cannot appeal the decision based on that evidence. You have to know the laws.

Before court, you may be obliged to go to mediation where you and the other side try to come to an agreement to prevent trial. If you are in a high conflict divorce, that may not be an option. I chose trial instead. Only 1-2% of divorce cases make it to trial and you may find yourself in this group of individuals. For me, I chose trial because the other side was dead set on me not being able to see my son and I need him to know when he gets to be old enough that his dad fought for him.

It's not going to be easy and no side will end up happy; prepare yourself! Mentally, physically and emotionally, because trust me, it is going to be draining. Just remember tough times never last, but tough people do. It's these times when you find out you are stronger than you ever could imagine. It's through these tough times that true character is built. Make sure to read some stoic quotes, and often, to help give you the strength to press forward.

Private Investigators

I wanted to include a small section on private investigators, as they may be an avenue to aid you, depending on your exact situation. There are a couple of types of Private Investigators: the old school ones who will track someone's movements and habits doing detective work in their vehicle and the type that does digital investigation. Get to know the ones in your area and check out the different services and costs involved. Most Private Investigators take their work very seriously and want to do their part in uncovering the truth, no matter how horrid that truth may be.

If you have a feeling your partner or ex-significant other is doing something they shouldn't be, you're probably right. Trusting your gut is very important, and knowing the truth can bring about peace of mind. Peace of mind is priceless, but know this, Private Investigators are expensive. Just one night could cost you $1.5k or more. It's up to you to decide if the potential dirt that could be uncovered is worth the cost.

It's also important to note that you cannot be your own investigator. You must know this! Doing so can lead to severe legal consequences for charges of stalking or worse. Not only that, anything you find will not be admissible in court. For your evidence to be admissible, it must come through a Private Investigator. I will tell you this, what my P.I. uncovered gave me peace of mind in knowing that my gut instincts were spot on and that I wasn't being paranoid. To me, just knowing that my gut feeling was correct made it worth the cost.

Drug and Alcohol Testing

If you are in a high-conflict divorce involving children, there is a very good chance that drug testing will be involved. My suggestion is that if you use any illicit substances, even marijuana, you stop immediately. Depending on the type of test you submit to, there could still be traces in your system for many months. We are covering this topic here for those of you in this situation who know the other party is abusing substance(s).

There are many types of drug tests that can be performed, each with their own pros and cons and knowing what you have available to you is important. We'll start with the good old urinalysis. Pretty much anyone can beat these things. My ex used to brag about being able to beat any urine test and so far, she has proven herself correct. My guess is from purchasing QCarbo32 from a local drug store. She has also come up with a dilute test. This is where there is too much water in the urine for the analyst to get an accurate result. You have negative dilute, meaning no drugs found, and positive dilute, meaning drugs were found, but the specimen was still diluted.

I was told by a local drug counselor that it was impossible to get a dilute test from just drinking water and wanted to prove that to myself considering my ex had just submitted a negative dilute sample. I'm going to tell you that it really isn't that hard. At the time, all I was drinking was water anyway. At my previous test, the sample appeared dilute by my own visual inspection, but there were no problems. However at my next test, the sample came back dilute. I had drank 3 bottles of water that day along with two energy drinks. I probably had my usual gallon of water the day prior and not much for dinner. I will say however that although the other side probably were given the results stating negative dilute, my sample was positive dilute, as it did show the current medication I take for Adult ADHD. That's another thing, maybe you know they have certain prescriptions and that they abuse them? Well, the courts count that as drug abuse and therefore forbidden. The problem is, and I hate to say it, but proving abuse of prescription medication will be close to impossible to prove, as the testing facilities don't report actual concentrations to you, just pass or fail.

If you are going to have the other party submit to one of these tests, I suggest finding a facility that requires direct observation. Doing this will prevent the other party from bringing in someone else's urine or that fake urine you can buy online and putting it into the specimen jar. You can normally request one of these tests no more than once per thirty days. You can choose a 5-panel or 10-panel and include ETG testing as well. One thing that really surprised me was that with the 10-panel that included opiates, the drug of choice for many, they didn't even test for the normal opiates like Hydrocodone that is commonly available to its users. For those you had to pay extra for a panel of expanded opiates. Nonsensical!

As for ETG, it is a metabolite your body creates while processing alcohol. They claim it can be detected in urine up to 80 hours after ingestion. I have also read that the 80 hour claim is something they use to sell the test. If you know that your ex was drinking around your children, have them submit to this test immediately. I'll get to how to make sure you can do that shortly.

The other types of tests are much more expensive, but can detect drugs in the system for a much longer period of time. They are the hair test and the nail test. Both are hard to beat. There are many places that sell products that claim to beat a hair test, but I don't know if any of them actually work. The ones I read about also require a long regime of using their product daily over many days. As for the nail test, the main drawback is that they will need to collect a good amount of nails, and the nails can't have anything like nailpolish applied. As for the frequency, depending on your local laws, you can normally request one of these tests every 90 days.

The way requesting a test normally works is like this; you purchase the test, then send confirmation of the purchase to the other party. The other party then has a set amount of time to submit a sample. If they don't submit a sample within that time frame, they are deemed to have failed the test. Should they pass the test, you are stuck with the bill, but if they fail it, they owe you the money you paid. During my divorce, I was in a unique situation. I had to pay for all the testing, no matter if she failed or not. I passed all my tests; she cannot say the same. Eventually at the final hearing the normal rules were granted.

If you are in a high-conflict divorce, stay away from drugs and alcohol. Even those few beers you may have in the evening to reward yourself for a hard day's work. I hope this isn't the case, but if your ex is using drugs while caring for your children, you must do everything you can to have them tested. This will be of use in the courtroom should you be able to prove it. Lastly, do not, under any circumstances, spy on your ex or have someone else spy on your ex. This is stalking and will be used against you, only a professional Private Investigator can legally perform this task. If your friend is out and sees them using or heard it through the grapevine, that is okay, the information is invaluable to you, and you should use it to the best of your ability to create an advantage. If you have hired a P.I., definitely share this information with them. If not, be sure to take notes and build your list of witnesses.

Division of assets

During my final divorce hearing, the opposing attorney made an attempt to chastise me for not having a joint bank account allowing my wife full access to family funds. When I was asked why this was the case, my answer was spot on, "I've been married before." That answer instantly shut down this particular line of questioning. Just can't argue with life experience.

I'm going to tell you this bluntly. Never, under any circumstances, allow your wife full access to your money. If you are both working and want to have a joint account you each pay into for bill payments, you can do that, but I would still suggest you don't. If you do though, make sure you have other accounts and investments that she can't touch.

I say this for multiple reasons. Most importantly you need to think about your future and if you have children, their future as well. Any decent man with kids will want to leave his kids better off than he was and the only way to do this is through smart investing and ensuring no one in this world can drain your funds.

The simple fact is that many people can't manage money, especially if they have a drug dependency. It's gone as soon as it hits their account. For women who have money management issues, it will go something like this. There's always going to be some new pair of shoes or clothing or makeup she just has to have. Expensive stylists, manicures, pedicures, spa days or the expensive girls' night out, where she is doing who knows what. The list goes on, but I'm sure you get the picture.

I know I would happily provide my ex-wife with just about anything she could ask for, whether it be something she just had to have, an expensive gift for her mom or family member, a trip to an Eagles concert with her brother, or the baby playpen we bought for her friend who just had another child she couldn't afford, but I would have been a fool to give her access to everything.

She proved this point when she forced me to give her an "allowance." I looked at it more as a budget. Okay, she wanted money every time I got paid, even though she had a small limit credit card I paid off each month? She simply needed to learn to manage that money better, consider it a budget and when it's gone, there will be no more until I get paid again. That money flew out of the purse as soon as it went in. Like clockwork, I kid you not.

Money is tricky, and you have to learn to manage it. I am not a financial manager and this is not financial advice, just this one man's opinion. Read books and study about growing your net worth. Maybe start with *Rich Dad, Poor Dad* by Robert Kiyosaki and go from there. Spend less than you earn. Cost dollar average into investments with a part of every dollar you make. After time, you will see those accounts grow. You also have to diversify. As they say, never put all your eggs in one basket.

If you have a good brain for numbers, start learning about the markets and how to do technical analysis. Learn about indicators, trend lines and chart patterns. Take a little money and use it as a test. Once you're making consistent gains, put in a little more. Rinse and repeat. Just remember, with anything you invest, you must be prepared to lose your entire investment. Don't put in more than you can afford to lose. This is a marathon, not a sprint. Don't expect to get rich overnight, that's not how wealth is created.

Children

They don't say "momma's baby, daddy's maybe" for nothing. This is an unfortunate reality in our current court system. If you are a man going through a high-conflict divorce, chances are that you will lose access to your children. There was a time when I could no longer endure the emotional abuse my wife constantly doled out, so I contacted a divorce attorney. This attorney gave me the best advice I ever received in regards to divorce.

He told me, you can't divorce your wife. Your child is under 3 years of age; she is going to take half of everything you own and you won't get to see your son. He told me to tough it out and just make sure there was no domestic violence. The point here is that this attorney was spot on. To a point. I still think I would have been better advised to secure a temporary order of protection based on severe emotional abuse.

Different states have different laws regarding child access in relation to their age. In Texas, if your child is under 3, you will barely get to see him or her and then you will go to what they deem a standard possession schedule, where you see your child every other week for a few days. The legislators' intention was for that schedule to be a minimum, but judges use it as a standard. The judges presiding over family courts in the state of Texas should be ashamed. I just had to say it. There will be different laws in your state and I highly suggest becoming familiar with them.

The courts claim they are looking out for the best interest of the child, but that is just words on paper. They really don't care about actual best interests. They just want to get you through the system, off their docket, and steamroll you if you happen to be a male. A man to the court system is nothing but a wallet. It's a sad reality, but you need to trust me on this.

That being said, you still have obligations to your child, and you need to make sure your child is well taken care of. Do your best to keep current on child support and if you can't, then make sure you pay at least something. Without payment, they can take you to jail and set bond for your arrears or money you owe. The unfortunate fact here is that all the money in the world won't turn a high-conflict woman into a good mom. You've got to fight. You will hit many dead ends, but for your kids, you have to keep trying. Believe me, I know, it seems like a losing battle, and it normally is, but you need to know, and when they are of age, your children need to know that their dad fought for them and did all he could to protect their well-being.

Another harsh reality is that unless you can prove your ex has a bad substance abuse issue or married a sex offender, you barely have a leg to stand on. The good news is that you will get to see your children, even if only every other Saturday for a few hours. That's a tough pill to swallow at first, and yeah, you're going to be pissed about it, but you have to make sure you don't mess up these visitations. Remember, you are there for your kids, don't allow the toxicity of your ex to mess up the precious moments you get with your kids. Not only will that hurt you in the long run, it will really affect the young ones, who are nothing but innocent victims of circumstance.

On the other hand, if your ex is refusing to allow you time demanded by the court, you get her ass back in court shouting parental alienation from the rooftop! That's metaphorical of course, never raise your voice in court. In court, you need to show absolute respect to not only the judge, but to the opposing side.

They may very well try to turn your kids against you, turn your friends against you, do whatever they can to assassinate your character, but stand strong. Even though your kids may carry life-long trauma and need tons of therapy to overcome having a high-conflict mother, they are your kids, and they need to know you will be there for them through thick and thin. Let them know this through any means necessary; legally that is.

Lastly, on the topic of your children, I want to mention an absolutely disgusting reality. There is a very probable chance that a high-conflict individual will weaponize their own children. They will use their own offspring for evil, and in many different ways. They will often try to make you emotional by turning your kids against you through lies and manipulation and any other sick way you can imagine. Prepare yourself for this. It certainly isn't right, by any means, but it's a reality. Again, you can't control their actions, only how you react. Make sure to document this. It's really all you can do. Well almost; I don't think it would hurt to send up a prayer. Children come first! Never lose sight of that fact.

How to Keep Your Head Up and Mind Right

Going through a high-conflict divorce of any nature will place a tremendous strain on any person, especially those of us who are quite empathetic. It's good to have some techniques at hand to help you keep your head up and your mind right. I thought this may be a good point to go over some of the feelings that may arise and how to deal with them.

First, you have to accept whatever it is as your new reality. You are here now, this is your life. They talk about the stages of acceptance as starting with denial, then moving to anger. If you find you may be in the anger stage, there is one thing that I beg you to remember; you can't change the other person's actions, but you do get to choose your response. Be very careful how you respond. Emotional outbursts do not lend themselves to your cause. Read about and learn BIFF to formulate your responses. Be brief, informative, friendly and firm.

The next stage in acceptance is depression. If you find yourself wrapped in self-pity and agonizing depression, learn to practice mindfulness and remind yourself of everything you still have that you are grateful for. I promise, if you really give it some thought, you will find something in your life that will lend itself towards gratitude.

The next stage is bargaining. You may find yourself remaining in the past, bargaining with the pain in an attempt to negotiate the hurt away. Again, you have to understand this is your reality and move forward so you can finally come to acceptance. It's very important you get to the acceptance stage as quickly as you can. It's only from there you can start moving forward.

Try to find a support network; a group of people that you can lean on for emotional assistance. This can be just hanging out, venting, or doing activities you enjoy in a group setting. If you don't have a support network, it's important you find one. My support network is actually rather small, it's mainly my Uncle Craig. He drives me crazy at times, but having him around has helped push me through the struggle. I also have a small group of really good friends that I don't get to see in person that often, but they have been there for me and helped me deal with losing my child and facing severe criminal charges from false allegations. I have also recently started attending weekly meetings with an organization called Women Against False Allegations. They are related to the National Coalition for Men. I am immensely grateful to each of them for the help and support they have given me through these tough times.

Along with your support network, there is some advice I am compelled to share with you. This is serious! Stay off social media. Everything you post or respond to can and very likely will be used against you in court. This goes for not only you, but your inner circle. Ask all to refrain from posting anything related to your situation, including responding to any online drama your spouse creates. I promise you, this will aid your cause.

We've already discussed therapy. If you believe that may help you, there are many resources out there. One that I liked was a therapist from BetterHelp.org. I saw this therapist before my divorce and was made to quit by my now ex-wife. She thought it was stupid and a waste of money that I talked to someone online to help digest my situation. Well, that was the reasoning she gave me. It's now obvious this was controlling behavior. Regardless, talking to a therapist may be a good way to gain some perspective and techniques for dealing with any pain from which you certainly suffer.

No matter how destructive your marriage and divorce were, remember that it is in the past, and now you have the opportunity to redefine yourself. Focus on healthy relationships and rebuild those you deem valuable that may have suffered through this process.

What now?

You may be asking yourself, "how do I avoid getting myself in a situation like this again?" Being able to discern a person's character is key to avoiding these situations. It's sad to say that in today's world, many people lack character. This goes for both men and women. On the flip side of the coin, there are still many out there who possess outstanding character. It's hard to discern one from another. You have to pay attention to red flags. I would even suggest journaling them.

We all, or at least most of us, seek friendships and love from others. This is an area where we must tread with utmost care. The sad reality is that the world is fraught with wolves in sheep's clothing. Spotting them is difficult to say the least. I'm not going to tell you what to do with your life. I'm assuming you're an adult and can make your own decisions, but I will say that I would not marry or cohabitate again. At least for a very long while. Should I ever find a person whom I would want to share the rest of my life with, I would first get an attorney to protect my assets and children. Then I would enroll us in couples therapy from the start.

A lot of us go running into relationships full speed with blinders on. This could be a form of hamartia. That fatal flaw that leads to downfall. Carefully vet anyone before allowing them into your life. Keep your inner circle small. If you are in the throes of a high-conflict divorce, I can tell you this; you will find out who your friends are, and you will find out that they number far less than you previously thought. Yet another sad reality, your friends are quite often not your friends. The police are certainly not your friends, but that is for another guide, I just wanted to throw it out there in hopes of helping someone in the future.

Learn to love yourself. This is a must. If you want to love others and help others, you must love and help yourself first. The path to self-love is probably different for each of us, but I urge you to find that path and start walking. Learning to love yourself is going to benefit you more than anything I can think of. Definitely more than winning the lottery. I don't know if you have seen the stories of those whose lives were ruined by an onslaught of money. If you look at each of those cases, you can find a couple of common denominators: they didn't know who their friends were, and they normally lacked true love for themselves. If you love yourself there is nothing anyone can say to you that will break you. You can get hate from all angles, yet you have bathed in metaphorical RainX and that hate just beads up and rolls off.

I apologize for profanity in what I am about to use. Pardon my French, so to speak. I normally try to keep profanity off my tongue, but I believe it is warranted here. One thing I like to believe is that a person needs to have a lot of fuck it in their attitude. Fuck you and what you say. You bring hatred towards me, you demean me for any reason, you go around town and speak negative words about me? Fuck it! Fuck you and what you say, I'm not going to let it affect me. Think of me what you will. I know me. I'm a good man. I care for others and have shown that throughout my 40 years on this planet.

Most importantly, I'm a great dad. I love my son more than anything in this world and when I hold him, when I play with him, when he naps on my shoulder, I know he feels the love I have for him. He is my life!

Everything I do, I do for him. Why? Because I'm his dad and that's my job. A job I perform with pride and consider myself lucky to possess.

Hopefully, something in this guide has helped you through these tough times or helped you avoid them all together. I love each and every one of you, and thank you for your support. If you would like to support me further, just want to chat, have any questions or whatever, feel free to reach out and contact me. You can email me at tbenfitz@gmail.com. I will do my best to help in any way I can.

To end, there is one thing I want to say and make known. **Daddy's coming son, daddy is doing the best he can, and daddy will always be here for you.**